preverbs

speaking animate

preverbs

George Quasha

BETWEEN
EDITIONS

Between Editions are published by Station Hill of Barrytown, 120 Station Hill Road, Barrytown, NY 12507, as a project of The Institute for Publishing Arts, Inc., a not-for-profit, Federally tax-exempt organization, 501(c)(3), in Barrytown, New York.

www.stationhill.org

Designed by Susan Quasha in collaboration with the author
Front cover: Axial Drawing from the Dakini Series [#1, 3-12-12, 43"×40"] by George Quasha

ISBN: 978-1-58177-136-7

Printed in the United States of America

for Robert Kelly

speaking animate

The trouble with paradise is you never want to be away from home.

I make what calls me out.
All gone before you know it.

Words may drop passing color yet seeing you here now are born again, and again.
Closing a word in the mouth feels the sound until the tongue can't stay still.

To unmask is to go silent.
Language makes no promise to communicate.

An articulated sound has it own dream in the ear.
Her presence in the room gives aroma to the syllables I voice.

Now she's ready to draw eros from foreign bodies.
It starts by focusing on the sounds beyond hearing, still felt.

By *she* I mean who speaking *animate* configures.
This is the time of alternative obscurities to see through.

Through thoroughly, as a word weighs.

They're playing the perfect music for our movie, *Rushing to Meet Anima*.
The rhythm's spacious enough I slip in the back door without a trace.

The drama is gathering soundless. It lives like that.
I never let go of her hand in my other world.

This I learn from you who read me back.

They say ancient Irish saw serpents where there aren't any.
I descend from there to here where I see what I say even unsounding.

Writing I extinguish my voice but there's calling you hear.

Falling apart is syntactic.
Writing at the edge of collapse is surrender.

Saying depths in a tongue all hands puts the cards on the table over the edge.
Time to stop asserting order where it's already in waiting.

Write this off as of a poet or one inspired by being written through.

A sacred grove takes refuge in the voice.

A language hasn't come through to itself if being inside isn't self-instructive.
Syllable by syllable earwise spreading orders the cells.

What configures signs, time switching subjects on the line like my life.
It seems the same is saying there were no same.

A journey ever worth taking records itself within your hearing even now.
"I will always have been here before with or without you."
Gnoaxial poetics, for want of right naming, finds pulse in grammatical drift.

The more she says the more I find configures.
The new singular noun soon plurals.

I'm beginning to recall the forgotten adventure, long since signed for.
The time of our playing recalls us back together.

This very time turns into space in our search for self true north.
Her tone is dissecting the next move out before.

The tense is two timing us.

The experience beyond reportable experience is self sensing.
Real work is indefensible.

Now to dowse the poetics of the poem to come.

We hold these principles to be self evident—in order to be self evidence.

Configuration is parthenogenetic.

We're talking fate here.

High flying biology. Bios mating logos.

Flowering, percipiently imaginarily auto-erotically speaking.

It sees and knows what it's doing not a moment before.

We call back to our other us through the air pressed into sound.

I'm just trapping animal life in its resound here.

Our group gives the dream time.

A date's charge belongs at heart to anytime.

Our only mythical bird is fleeing the page as we speak.

It makes a very very very fast line out.

Sculpting hands in the saying.

Not every finger is instantly intelligible.

Signing principle, it calls itself, and hands itself over.

Watching your dancing feet is its own dance.

What if everyone talked funny at once.
I'm willing to avoid special pleading but ignored distractions will have their say.

Sudden behaviors may be of unaccountable origin.
Tongue the surface long enough and you bleed old demons long in exile.

Learn from the dog to dig up old shame, then bury it where you want it.
If you find a guy's personality be sure to send it back.

Meet you where we know each other.

Beautiful music takes me away rather than throwing me further in.
Clamoring lines cannot disguise the sound of one mind slipping.

The center is holding just fine, yet the periphery is forgetting where it is.

Freudian slips of the hand put your mouth on your money.
Also note paradisal memes at the tip of the slip.

Life goes on … off … on … off.

What am I hearing with these other ears?

Prepare your mouth with pre-carnal intentions.
Poetry valorizes childhood because children make language.

First language.
It gets you little again to be verbal.

I can't deny my excitement upon reaching the threshold of carnality.
No more hovering over secondhand bodies.

The heart is the organ of consorting.

Life is intelligent means it knows where it's going but I don't.
Fearful asymmetry.

Contacting the word's core intent to mean itself is poetic insistence.
Logophagi know that certain morphemes are more delicious than others.

No truth behind the poem, only forward in its own before.

I'm scared sacred.

The threshold of panic is nearer than you think.
I see line as raft on which to contemplate the dangers of survival and not.

Mind turns all day long on feeling good about this or that.
Keep losing favorite images of myself: getting harder and harder to favor.

The earth does not fruitlessly give us her fruit.
Turn your back for a moment and another portion of Eternity is hiding in your mind.

Every forecast verbal order betrays its possible oracle in the wild.
The music undesigned by music is from the earth and feeds undefined needs.

No two sins are the same.
A reading here either tunes me back or unwinds me out.

Incarnation potentially is paradisiacal entering the paradipsychical.
It's time to pull your head back in between the letters.

Poetry marks the passing of time with lived-in beat, wording up and off, bounding.
Every thought rethinks reversing further.

Mind action a pulse felt in the telling's no easygoing equation.
The lump in the throat gets bumped up.

We mean to dissatisfy one tune at a time.

My date with Blake has brought me here.
I write his name now as never before.

It teaches me to do as I'm folded.
Nothing is the way it's always been said.

Working language means cutting through to secret holdings.
My stash of youth is long forgotten.

I have no idea what it is I'm doing, so I ask you to read me to me.
Slips of the ear show me my fear.

My goal is to be all here all the line.

I leave the tail behind to lighten the page.
I leave room for the animal's tale to renew.

Slips of the hand make me hear again.
I go dumb to enable speaking direct.

Youth of being is a work in ungress.
Now go home.

> "If all is illusion then the distinction illusion/reality is relatively useless."
> "Absolutely."
> ONTONONYMOUS THE PARTICULAR

A letter is a wand.

A word the bird let loose in whir.

A sentence a neighborhood to let mind range with over to there.

She dances beside herself.

This vision has no outside, no matter how many times it's said.

The pulse is in palettes and feet.

Sound you hear is from the bottom in its middle having grammar.

It makes sense the way it makes love.

I belong to her beside herself.

Tear along the line that has no other side.

I draw her moving as if drawing blood.

Thicker or thinner across the space depends on your pressing in and how far.

She startles herself out of oneness to excite her zero, loving her many.

Two dissimilar objects in the same frame resonate ownness.

The paradise that is not inside the voice has no song.

Imagine a world without first languages.
Struggles of the undertongue are accordingly allowed.

When the poet surrenders long enough language surrenders.

I can't stop my hawking attention to the charged thought entities in evidence.
Torsion saves us from believing where we are.

I want to eat her thought of herself at play in my image body.
I feel so close to her when she lets me say these things.

You should not believe anything I tell about her. It drives her away.
She's getting away! Start over: She *is* getting away. By her nature.

Poetic surprise is saying in which there is no gliding beyond the syllable.
A torqued word in the mouth is nature's tongue tuning.

I watch my hands lose things in plain sight.
The thrill of impermanence is theatrical.

Using your lingual reflex she lassoes your linguality well nigh bronco busting.
The tongue gets kicked around no matter what.

Earth talks dirty to distract me from counting the virtues of my day.
I'm left lusting in the sidelines.

My gender is feeling a little dizzy in here, pronouns adrift.

The path is a sudden curvilinear reach.
I'm on retreat from working intricacy inside the work.

Rushing forward here at any moment it's never too late to return and we do.
I do. I am a man who marries. It's how you say it to yourself.

Throttle the syllable when it asks for it.
It's the emphasis by retraction that gives the thing outline.

It has to deal with sudden emergence you can call visionary, if you see the point.
That's a figure of speech. It figures speaking and long legs ready to curve around.

It channels a further self still off yonder.
Therefore the lasso effect of the text. Suck back.

I can't tell you where it's starting and stopping, it's so life-like.
Enjoy the inevitable disorientation (she's watching from afar).

Confusion can come in pairs.
The number is no help except for the relief. Timely but temporary.

I'm seeing through clouds—can you tell?
Tell me, fold back the lips, there's unspeakable color to reckon with.

The poet opens small doors to her other worlds.
I watch work confusing gender, eroding priority.

A subsequent sigh is involuntary and therefore has keyed force.

I can't wait to contemplate these words at the end of the line.
I'm starting without you.

Contemplate our world allowing that its creator has a sense of ecstatic irony.
Perfection takes off the white gloves.

Clouds part.
Vision is a state in which a god knows you as it biblically were.

Shine through or see through or more.
Every two is manyer than you think and a splitting *y* in the middle.
We fork by nature.

We talk treasure down and dirty.
Till death do us art.

I admit to wanting to hold her hand while crossing.

This first line is an inexact repeat of a line to come.

Given that the earth's not round but spherical it's flattish from where I stand.
You can prove me wrong right now performing the indicative 1st person as you.
Equally true is the question how wrong can I be?

Earth claims person and gender in that we are.
I would know that voice on the phone no matter what.

Earth has a poetics with a noetics.
From ecodelia to glossodelia in single line bound.

In this measure poetry is irruptive.
An unauthorized line tap. No mercy.

This is an instance of a voice trying to get through without giving a name.
I couldn't wait to get home and throw open the brackets.

So much language is forgetting who it is.
Identity is evaporative at a certain temperature.

Language is child's play.
They'll say anything to get the attention saying deserves.

This fulfills the promise of the first line.

Possibly I can't stop remaking the world in her own image.

She is coded to chop logic like garlic.
It's more literal than literary, like garlic.

The line is introspecting upon itself.
How I know is going with the wide awake irreality of indefensible rhythm.

I think to hear what things think in me.
Surfacing against the grain thinking things can't see straight, let alone repeat right.

It tries to come through but I'm adrift in chronology.
Temporal feedback has underlogic.

The time based medium tells its own fortune.

Imagining going on forever without attachment is beyond imagination.
Like rearview backtracking with forward view the very line scans as it goes.

Lineal relation to the whole feeds on a sense of isolation felt in a crowd.
A midline crisis reflects changing subject midsentence with a straight face.

The line can't make up its mind but takes me here anyway.

The resident language is strictly autobiographical.

I leave content to the voyeur in me.
At a certain point in the story only leftovers will do.

My life story is at stake.
I'm left to hovering over scraps.

Poets and children at play love levitating agents.
Protectors of intelligential somniloquies are loving in silence.

Dante, Dante, para-Dante, parasomnial Dante, body of sweetheart.
Soul sought Avernus, spirits are at play like lines at bay.
The tone! The vowel! excited sounds leap from our scrapheap history.
Coffers, coffins, and other commonly sacred confines … think dictionary urns.

A word and her thing are non-separate in real talk.
Dogs bay at spirited sleep talk's diction fictions.
Time to let thinking marry her extradimensionals.

Just think! there are those who think emptiness thoughtless!
Registering the heart on full, champagne all around!

Enough does not readily apply to poetry and sex.

Lexical spaces are peepholes for those pressing from the other side.
Reading is being spied upon, dimensionally speaking.

And we wonder what is running what and who, whom.
Who knew in the big picture with the luminous sky the mushroom has an eye?

Thought forms traversing language dispose by attraction the matter in hand.
Word order guides mood weather.

Miming the poem, so to speak, life aware meditates itself.
I speak in analogy to the extent that things properly speaking compare; they don't.

I don't and I won't compare unless my spine lengthen and the vine stand straight.
A verse is the possibility of prefiguring what is actually happening as it turns out.

Only possible to study time from the perspective of the atemporal.
Poem time wells in semic spaces between, literally.

No telling what it'll tell next. It's not literature it's typing.
Always on time even when late or early bespeaks a throughsexed poetics.

No summaries.

Hope to repair wrecked train of thought.

Charlie Chan

Why do we want to be the covert choir of preaching poetry?

A soft word does not scratch the tongue.

She feels for you.

Or *it*, what only understands perfection precisely where it is, instantly.

Our minds are working side by side and word by word with breathing spaces.

Thinking listens up in her youthful instance.

Reading between reverbs. Body middles sound sense from the inside.

I is *going* for us both.

How talk it walking? in twos? plus ones?

You can put a poeia on the end of anything and we'll feel it.

Like penile nothing.

If you have time and space for it let it rip right through, readerly.

Reading descending. It's more than a sentence that goes down so far, and you in it.

Highly localized interiority is infrasyntactic.

It tracks language feeling for itself.

I celebrate the wobble in the middle.

It draws out the well of onliness.

Ancient ancestor once say, "Even wise man cannot fathom depth of woman's smile."

I'm feeling by ear.

Consider them gods and not cruel but ecstatic.

They have trick tongues and can't talk straight but use us as waves to curve words.

In this moment we are here for their ride. Climb on under.

Transport poetics in the transtraditionals, revering rumors revved high.

We ask forgiveness for poem talk. I'm on her knees.

She makes me say these things because she is a middle way like no other.

The method is to wear me down to a base line vital pulse.

Next pour right through carefully following the barely perceptible impulse.

Almost dreams the state resists the name but go ahead and call it poetic that flares.

Poetics remains neutral on its name but takes care when it comes to hers.

There's a watch out on her names.

It makes me wait until I have nothing else to fight with and then sets me loose.

When I think what is being said I get a lump in the stomach.

No go on the intellectual gizmo.

Yes on any kind of lift, free run, no drift, too swift, the actual thing getting a lift.

It hits the beat like rock bottom.

The tongue gets hands on quick.

The hearback suddenly gets high in the sense of crossing right on over.

I feel language like a woman.

What you read is what you get.

Easy to forget that even now the tongue is doing its dance of attraction, with veils.

Her smile talking says I'm a noun ready to verberate, so I'm here, on verbal crawl.

Tongue obsession follows radical inflection.

I'm not talking about something so much as reflecting it on bended knee.

Getting reports on language is a thriller.

A thing you know has already said itself, but testifying further is another matter.

Poetry is a life threatening force.

Getting a living chance to come through or not by speaking at the leaping point.

Poetics is indifferent to the outcome but not the come from.

Jesus fuckin' motherfuckin' Christ is now a term of exaltation excited beyond irony.

She kids me not the Magdalene.

Sine qua non of the mind gone sane.

I was not born to sing but apparently I'll risk singing to be born.

The right hand wouldn't understand what the left hand is doing even if it knew.

Fascination comprehends the days falling from me.

Syntax imitates this temporal bind. Ending in the middle.

Open to the end and over.

Opening the mouth lets out the whodunit, to whom who did what.

Birthing grammars.

I'm here on spec.

Some things get said to find out what it's like to be said.

The poetics of birthright is ever in a state of neglect on our planet.

We're sending out for alternatives.

Poetry experiments with the principle that if you can think a better place it can be.

The request comes from language itself bioprogrammed to optimize.

The claim is non-authorizing. It clamors.

The threat is that things will clear.

This in the wake of the words still falling from.

The whole thing said's verb.

Talking hands can't keep to themselves.

From the beginning is speaking on behalf of the truth in its unauthorized version.

The principle is if you know you know.

Declaring so presumes true things get a little early notice.

It's long known there's no sexual balance but only precarious rectification *now*.

I precisely cannot tell you how open I am meaning.

No lines link in the end. All lines do from the beginning.

Where she can't track it I can't hack it or didn't. Would not.

The voice from nowhere says *Confess in reverse.* No connectors.

I'm taking the way around, starting where I came through at the start.

There's an area deep inside that cannot refuse when asked.

Even a little attention attends avalanche.

Shave off some phonemic skin to get to a gnoseme.

It's time to invent reading commensurate to it's own undoing.

There's another side trying to get through wherever we stand in the way.

Coach wheels in old movies going both ways push time out into *our view*.

This is how it happens from then on.

Real life is not outside this book.

It feels to me that what is pushing in from the outside is myself.
The overthere is rising as we speak.

I am I that only can walk my plank.
The poet is the part of me that records the plash. Brave girl.

Born of knowing to know is rising to the occasion.
It figures it has a right.

Why bother figuring out what it's saying when you can't remember it anyway?
Take hold in flight.

The body forgetting itself remembers the world too much.
The face has grammar but hearing won't let me see it.

Declaration has more syntax than ever known and higher stakes.
It goes to the end of time which may or may not be now in the line.

I travel by night when there's not a lot of traffic.
Anything for a little more actual space in wording.

Who reads it reads death otherwise.

CODA

(tell-tail)

Let there be dark, she said it seems so lightly tunneling.

If you say it twice and it sounds right the door is open for a return.
Mind thunders until you hear perfectly.

No gospel is complete until denied and bastardized in strictly personal demotic.
Example: The one that is two is not a shoe.

As for the two speaking as one, what reading hears tell in the middle voice?
It is not the dark that darkens.

She came up behind to be his power and free him from it.
The music of anything said releases its truth.

For our word order minds what it does.
I sing for the one now going by in your eyes.

There is dark to see by.
Grammar opens backsides to let go who did what to whom.

She says I was *born mouthfirst* in Japanese here translated.
There is no natural speech.

Timing out, outing time, time present and time past, timely as the more they are.
Anything talks funny without listening.

On the count of three, spark.

The dark of which we cannot speak is scintillant.
I stand informed.

That at this moment you're not outside the book has zero metaphoric value.
Gratitude is due for trudging along at breakthought pace.

That axial irony's not contrary to straight across, you can take your tonic straight up.
Tonal tissue bounds the body of two.

I study relationships to know where I stand.
Mirror can't stop reflecting further, so we look on.

Word sites where tone writes.
The mouth knows its place, her place, your place all at once to recite further.

The echo bespeaks alternative intelligence.
It maps mind homeomorphic to the territory leading on, sound by syllable.

A bounding line registers levitational overflow in lineaments including desire.
Just talking the things that hold us together hold true.
It takes time to get young.

speaking animate

SUB-CONTENTS

George Quasha's poetry includes *Somapoetics* (1973), *Word-Yum* (*Somapoetics 64-69*) (1974), *Giving the Lily Back Her Hands* (1979), *Ainu Dreams* (1999), *Verbal Paradise* (*preverbs*) (2011), and *Scorned Beauty Comes Up From Behind* (*preverbs*) (2012). *Preverbs* has been a core poetic vehicle for some fifteen years and is currently structured as nine books, each with seven poem-complexes (series of varying length). The present work is a poem-complex from *Glossodelia Attract* (*preverbs*), forthcoming. His work, exploring principles in common within various mediums in addition to language, includes sculpture, drawing, video, sound, and performance, and his book *Axial Stones: An Art of Precarious Balance*, Foreword by Carter Ratcliff (2006), presents his work in axial sculpture, along with axial drawing and language. His work has been exhibited at the Baumgartner Gallery (New York), Slought Foundation (Philadelphia), the Samuel Dorsky Museum of Art (SUNY New Paltz), the Snite Museum of Art (Notre Dame), and elsewhere. The internationally exhibited video work *art is: Speaking Portraits* records over 1000 artists, poets, and musicians in eleven countries (saying what art/music/poetry is). Awarded a Guggenheim Fellowship in video art and an NEA Fellowship in poetry, he is the author of *An Art of Limina: Gary Hill's Works and Writings* (with Charles Stein) (foreword by Lynne Cooke) (2009). The anthology *America a Prophecy: A New Reading of American Poetry from Pre-Columbian Times to the Present*, co-edited with Jerome Rothenberg in 1973, has been reissued by Station Hill of Barrytown (SHP Archive Editions), of which he is co-founder/-publisher with Susan Quasha. He performs axial music both solo and in collaboration with Gary Hill, Charles Stein, and David Arner.

Continuing work appears at www.quasha.com.

This publication includes
34 numbered copies of a limited, signed edition,
including an original drawing.

Special thanks to
Susan Quasha
for the design of text and cover
using an axial drawing from the Dakini Series
by George Quasha.

The text was set in Electra,
with Centaur and Apolline titling.

CPSIA information can be obtained at www.ICGtesting.com
Printed in the USA
LVOW11s2139160416

483926LV00001B/7/P